a Franciscan Christmas

KATHLEEN M. CARROLL

FOREWORD BY JACK WINTZ, O.F.M.

ST. ANTHONY MESSENGER PRESS
Cincinnati, Ohio

Cover and book design by Mark Sullivan
Cover image © Chiff | Dreamstime.com
Interior illustrations © Lisa Thornberg | istockphoto.com

Scripture passages have been taken from *New Revised Standard Version Bible*, copyright
©1989 by the Division of Christian Education of the National Council of the
Churches of Christ in the U.S.A., and used by permission. All rights reserved.

LIBRARY OF CONGRESS CATALOGING-IN-PUBLICATION DATA
Carroll, Kathleen (Kathleen M.)
A Franciscan Christmas / Kathleen M. Carroll ; foreword by Jack Wintz.
p. cm.
ISBN 978-0-86716-986-7 (alk. paper)
1. Christmas. 2. Creches (Nativity scenes) 3. Francis, of Assisi, Saint, 1182-1226.
4. Christian life—Catholic authors. I. Title.
BV45.C328 2010
263'.915—dc22

2010035928

ISBN 978-0-86716-986-7

Published by St. Anthony Messenger Press
28 W. Liberty St.
Cincinnati, OH 45202
www.AmericanCatholic.org
www.SAMPBooks.org

Printed in the United States of America.

Printed on acid-free paper.

10 11 12 13 14   5 4 3 2 1

Contents

Foreword

The love and fascination I had for nature as a young boy in the Indiana woods stayed with me and grew even stronger during my years as a Franciscan student of philosophy and theology. I was always ready to set aside my college texts and go enjoy the book of nature—the trees and fields and brooks, the birds and other creatures found in the wooded areas of the property surrounding our seminaries in Michigan and Ohio.

Perhaps my own attraction to nature made me curious about Saint Francis' habit of calling his fellow creatures "brother" and "sister." The little saint went happily about the Italian countryside, calling out with affection to "Brother Sun" and "Sister Moon," to "Brother Fire" and "Sister Water," to "Sister Swallow" and "Brother Cricket," and so forth. What secret instinct or intuition, I wondered, led him to this easy, familial relationship with all creation? What fueled his vision of the universe as one happy, interconnected family?

First, I believe that Francis had an uncomplicated yet deep sense of the common goodness of creation because he saw it coming from the same good Creator. This, of course, made him a brother to all: If the marigold and the wolf had the same Father in heaven as he did, then quite simply, they were sister and brother to him.

More than this, it seems, the meaning of the Incarnation hit his imagination like a bombshell. Somehow he realized that when the Word entered the world of creation and became flesh, everything was profoundly changed. If God became a part of the created world in the birth of Jesus Christ, then the dignity of all creatures was raised dramatically to a new height. The original goodness of creation was reinforced a thousand times over when God waded into the stream of creation—into the realm of minerals and plants and animals, of snowflakes and rainstorms—and so entered the history of this planet.

Francis saw the world of matter and flesh in the same way—as if there is one stuff from which all things are made and which unites all creatures in solidarity, in one solid body of matter and flesh.

And Francis was deeply aware of one moment in history—the moment that God entered creation and the Word was made flesh.

For Francis this event sent shock waves through the whole network of dust and flesh. Not only was the human nature made holy by the Incarnation; the whole fabric of creation was also charged with the divine presence.

Francis sensed that all creation (not just humans) had been redeemed through the Incarnation. Did not John the Baptist proclaim in the words of Isaiah that "all flesh shall see the salvation of God" (Luke 3:6)? And did not Christ tell his followers to "proclaim the good news to the whole creation" (see Mark 16:15)? Why shouldn't Francis take this literally? Why shouldn't he preach to the birds and fishes and wolves? These are all part of the flesh, part of the brotherhood and sisterhood of creation. Francis refused to be a human chauvinist, pretending that he was saved apart from the rest of creation.

This is why the feast of Christmas meant so much to Francis and why he wanted the whole of creation to take part in the feast. History credits Francis of Assisi with beginning the tradition of the Christmas crèche. This popular custom goes back to the year 1223, when Francis invited the townspeople of Greccio, Italy, to come to a cave outside town and reenact the first Christmas.

The book you're holding uses the Christmas crèche as a lens for examining Franciscan spirituality. Just as Francis found a spark of the divine in every blade of grass, you are invited to find a deeper meaning in each element of the Nativity scene. In these pages you'll find a little bit of history, a dash of wit, and a chance to remember that the things that make Christmas special are available to us in all seasons.

May the spirit of Saint Francis bless you in this holiday and all year long.

—*Friar Jack*

Introduction

Near the tiny Italian town of Assisi stands a giant, magnificent church, Santa Maria degli Angeli, St. Mary of the Angels. The people from around the world who make pilgrimage to this site are impressed by its many altars, with Mass being said almost constantly at one or more. They can easily find among its many confessors someone who speaks their language (or, if they prefer, someone who does not). The grandeur of the building is remarkable, even in a country rich with spectacular churches.

What truly sets this church apart is a small chapel, the Portiuncola. Many great cathedrals have chapels along their walls or on other levels of the building, but the Portiuncola is set in the center of the church, directly under the massive dome. This humble structure—too small to be a one-car garage—was the original St. Mary of the

Angels, so named by the saint of Assisi, Francis. This is where he gathered his brothers, his minor friars, to worship in the early days of the Franciscan Order.

Though there are other sites associated with these early days of Franciscan spirituality, this is the setting that expresses in stone and stained glass the essence of this book. Just as the Portiuncola nestles quietly amid the magnificence of a huge basilica, the Christmas crèche occupies a similarly humble position in most homes. It may be found beneath a grand evergreen, decked in gold and lights. Perhaps it's on a mantle, barely noticeable above a roaring fire. Maybe it's even on a corner table, protected from tiny hands, but also obscured from view. But wherever it is found, however it seems to be outshined by grander decorations, it is the reason for the rest.

The Christmas crèche is especially suited to a conversation about Franciscan spirituality because it was Francis himself who, though he would humbly deny it, popularized the tradition. A description of that first Nativity scene in the mountains at Greccio is captured by Bonaventure in one of his biographies of Francis:

> Three years before he died St. Francis decided to celebrate the memory of the birth of the Child Jesus at Greccio, with

the greatest possible solemnity. He asked and obtained the permission of the pope for the ceremony, so that he could not be accused of being an innovator, and then he had a crib prepared, with hay and an ox and an ass. The friars were all invited and the people came in crowds. The forest reechoed with their voices and the night was lit up with a multitude of bright lights, while the beautiful music of God's praises added to the solemnity. The saint stood before the crib and his heart overflowed with tender compassion; he was bathed in tears but overcome with joy. The Mass was sung there and Francis, who was a deacon, sang the Gospel. Then he preached to the people about the birth of the poor King, whom he called the Babe of Bethlehem in his tender love.

A knight called John from Greccio, a pious and truthful man who had abandoned his profession in the world for love of Christ and was a great friend of St. Francis, claimed that he saw a beautiful child asleep in the crib, and that St. Francis took it in his arms and seemed to wake it up.

The integrity of this witness and the miracles which afterwards took place, as well as the truth indicated by the vision itself, all go to prove its reality. The example which Francis put before the world was calculated to rouse the hearts of those who are weak in the faith, and the hay from the crib, which was kept by the pole, afterwards cured sick animals and drove off various pestilences. Thus God wished to give glory to his servant Francis and prove the efficacy of his prayer by clear signs.[1]

For many holy men and women, there is one aspect of the Christian faith that holds special significance. Saint Norbert was enthralled by the Eucharist; Paul by spreading the Word; Ignatius of Antioch wanted nothing so much as martyrdom. For Francis of Assisi, all the magic and mystery of the faith was best summed up in the Incarnation. The very *fact* of Jesus, of God become man, transformed all of creation. If Jesus was wholly divine and wholly human, then human beings were indescribably elevated. If Jesus was a baby lying in a crib of straw, then straw, and cribs, and the animals surrounding him, and all the things of our world, were created anew. The world around us was no longer a land to which we were banished because of our sin; it was what it was always meant to be—the best of all possible worlds, crafted solely for our benefit. The animals, the rocks and trees, even the sun and moon, were our brothers and sisters.

Franciscan author Ilia Delio provides a more structured insight into the meaning of the Incarnation for Francis:

> First…Francis perceived that the world is good and provides for authentic human needs. While the world is filled with God's overflowing goodness, it is poverty that allows one to experience this goodness by becoming radically dependent on God. Second, for Francis the meaning of creation and thus of the human person is revealed and manifest in Jesus Christ. It is in and through Christ that Francis discovers the meaning of his own life, the dignity of the human person, and the goodness of creation. Finally Francis [realized] that the human person, like Christ, is fragile, limited and vulnerable. Francis himself grew in compassionate love, like Christ, willing to give his life for the sake of the other. These three aspects of Francis' "evangelical world view" (creation, Incarnation, human person) all point to the fact that, for Francis, the human person is the fundamental category of experience. It is the person of Jesus Christ who reveals to him the dignity of all persons and that of creation itself. For Francis, the only "work" that is fundamental to his way of life is to imitate Christ and to make

that experience of Christ available to others. Evangelical life focuses on what we are, not what we do.[2]

This focus on the true meaning of things, on what we are rather than on what we do, is what the Christmas crèche—all of Christmas, in fact—is all about. Jesus was in a manger outside of Bethlehem sanctifying all of creation, not because of anything he did, but just because he was there, being who he was in that time and place.

The best Christmases of our lives have nothing to do with how big the tree is, or whether we have one at all. The best ornaments are not those priceless heirlooms we pack away with care each year and anxiously unwrap to see if they've survived another year in storage; they are the tattered handiwork of children and grandchildren, made with crayon, glitter, or toilet paper tubes and pasted with tiny photos of tiny faces we can barely remember. Their value is in the memories they stir, the stories told and retold over a score of holidays, the rediscovered closeness—or sometimes just the memory of that closeness—of those we love.

This Christmas, as you wrestle with tangled lights and strained finances, remember to put all that aside and focus on the true meaning of the day. It can be found in a tiny house and in the love of all those gathered there.

CHAPTER ONE

Jesus

In the beginning was the Word, and the Word was with God, and the Word was God. He was in the beginning with God. All things came into being through him, and without him not one thing came into being. What has come into being in him was life, and the life was the light of all people. The light shines in the darkness, and the darkness did not overcome it.

—John 1:1—5

*I*n the Nativity scene at my childhood home, Jesus was a fixture—and not just metaphorically. He was of a piece with the plaster straw-filled crib he rested in, and securely fastened to the middle of the little wooden shack that sheltered him. Setting up the Nativity scene was a three-part process: (1) remove from box; (2) blow off dust; (3) put it somewhere. That somewhere was under the tree until one year when a bumper crop of presents claimed Saint Joseph's head as a casualty. The tragedy was neatly resolved when my father's prized West Point mug, with a cadet for a handle, suffered damage of its own. In subsequent years, we added a fourth step to setting up the crèche—(4) cram cadet head into Saint Joseph's neck hole—and displayed the charming travesty on the fireplace mantel.

The first time I saw a Fontanini Nativity set, I was dumbfounded. All those beautiful (and expensive) pieces! There were the old standbys I knew well—Mary, Joseph, Jesus, a few shepherds, a handful of farm animals—but also a cast of characters new to me.

There were villagers and angels and the three kings and more and more. I remember scouring my illustrated Bible to find mention of some of these more obscure characters—did the Magi really have servants?—and having little success. I started looking for the crèche at friends' homes. Each was different. Why were some plain white porcelain and others multicolored plastic? Why were some so sparsely populated (think *Waiting for Godot*) while others had a cast of dozens (think *Les Miserables*)? I didn't want to distinguish myself as having any particular interest in religious matters, but I began to pry. I found that my friends' thoughts on the Nativity scene were as diverse as the items themselves. Some put out the Nativity scene and held off on all other holiday decorations until Christmas Eve. Some set up the crèche but withheld the baby Jesus until Christmas Day. One family even had a tradition of moving the pieces around the house. Jesus would start out on a windowsill and end up in the crib Christmas morning, while the long-traveling wise men would hide out on the back porch until they showed up on Epiphany. I began to think that my own family, with its cadet-headed Joseph, could stand to take its faith a bit more seriously.

Of course, in any Nativity scene there are some nonnegotiable characters. And whether he waits in his crib from the first day of Advent or shows up with the gifts Santa leaves, the star of the show is Jesus.

Some forward thinking municipalities hang street banners to proclaim to us the need to remember the "reason for the season." But such quiet voices outside of church, and the even quieter voices inside, can scarcely be heard among the commercial pitches that offer quite a different message. This is the season, they tell us, for proving your worth to others by giving them just the right gift in just the right package. This is the season for telling others precisely how much we love them. (Precisely. There's even a gift receipt inside the box in case you weren't sure if it was on sale.) It's that magical time of year when you remember last year's socks and decide that Grandma would be just as happy with a nice card. It is the season for letting children everywhere know, in the words of one billboard, that "Santa likes rich kids better than poor kids."

We know in our heads that Jesus is the reason for the season, but we feel in our hearts that this is another test we cannot pass, another grand effort that will result in someone's disappointment. Christmas is a hurdle, often an insurmountable one. For families with small children, it is a test of whether we can do better than our parents, if they disappointed us, or as well as our parents, if they set an impossible standard. It is a time that stretches every budget and every schedule and strains every nerve. For those in their older years it is a challenge to pull it off one more time, or a challenge to forget disappointments of years past, or a challenge to distract ourselves from thinking of those who won't be gathering with us this year because we've lost them—to death, to other spouses, to young families of their own, to a quarrel that has gone on far too long. And for children—all our focus—it is a time to be afraid of asking too much, to be ashamed of receiving too little, to wish they had something to give.

Christmas is a time of joy, but all too often it is a manufactured joy, made up of food, gifts, decorations, cards, family visits, special outfits, indulgent confections, and spectacular messes of gift wrap and dirty dishes. Advent is no longer a time of joyful waiting, but an item on the to-do list: Wreath? Check. Candles? Check. And church on Christmas? Well, yes, we simply must, but it has to be after the children are dressed, but before they've eaten anything to spoil their new outfits, and we'll need to schedule a visit to Grandma and Grandpa while they're still presentable, but they'll want their presents first and…. How about Midnight Mass? Yes, beautiful, quiet, and prayerful, but followed by an all-night session with a two-hundred piece some-assembly-required something-or-other and the joy of Christmas morning seen through one bloodshot eye over a steaming mug of caffeine.

How can Jesus help us with all of this? Here's a start. Open the Gospels and read the Nativity story in Luke. When I was looking for all those superfluous Fontanini characters in my Bible, they weren't there. And guess what else wasn't there? Christmas trees. New outfits. Gift wrap. It may shock you to know that the word "Macy's" does not appear once in the Bible. And that Santa character? Nope.

Before you get caught up in the madness that is Christmas in America, or even if you're already caught up in it, take a break. Take a few minutes to remember who Jesus was, and what he was about. This is something Francis never forgot. As Murray Bodo describes it:

> Everything Francis does or says has its center in Jesus. He embraces himself and others because he has first embraced the Lord, whose love makes it possible for Francis to reach out, even to what is repulsive in himself and others. It is Jesus who shows Francis what it means to overcome shame: For the divine nature was his from the first; yet he did not think to snatch at equality with God, but made himself nothing, assuming the nature of a slave (Philippians 2:7). It is Jesus who eats with publicans

and sinners, who lives as a carpenter, whose disciples are by and large poor men and women. It is Jesus who has nowhere to lay his head and who dies on a cross, stripped even of the clothing of his self-respect.

It is impossible to overemphasize the centrality of Jesus…in the life of Saint Francis.[1]

That first Christmas in Bethlehem is the only time in the Gospels Jesus gives anyone a Christmas gift—and that gift is himself. The magic and mystery of that gift is that, in sharing his life and his own divine and human nature with us, Jesus gives us the gift of ourselves. He helps us become the people we were always meant to be—sons and daughters of the most high God.

If we want to follow Francis' example, we will follow Jesus'. The first and most precious gift we can give anyone is the gift of our time—after all, we only have so much of it. And we have far less of it if we are scrambling to get gifts of less value. I spent a lot of evenings working a second job at Christmastime so the kids would have gifts under the tree, but I now wonder if they would have needed those game systems, those music players, those DVDs, if they had had a mother at home every night. Try to set thoughts of presents aside and focus on presence. Who wants and needs more of your time? Your children? Your parents? Siblings, neighbors, coworkers?

When else does Jesus give a gift? His first miracle, at the wedding at Cana, is turning water to wine to help a young couple celebrate their wedding. One way to follow this example is to give someone six hundred gallons of wine, but I suspect there are better ways to help others navigate the milestones in their lives. Someone you know is celebrating Christmas for the first time in a new home or with a new baby. Someone else may be living through the season for the first time without a spouse, a child, or even a pet.

When Jesus fed the multitudes, he didn't call a caterer or cook for three days. He took what was available and made it work. Maybe this year's Christmas feast is a potluck on paper plates. Maybe it's at your church or a local shelter after serving others in the community. Think about those who might not have family nearby. Is there room for them at your table?

As for all the other trappings of Christmas? Of course there's room for beautiful decorations, lovely gifts, and nice clothes, but remember how all these things got their start. Santa Claus was once Saint Nicholas. One of the less gruesome tales told about this saint involves a poor farmer with three daughters. In ancient times, daughters were a liability in an agrarian society—they could not do the heavy work of a son and could not be married off without a dowry. Knowing the farmer's circumstances, Nicholas threw three bags filled with gold coins (or golden balls, depending on the storyteller) through an open window, providing for each daughter's dowry without embarrassing their father by making his poverty known. The golden balls were memorialized by hanging oranges as decorations, and the generous gesture was remembered by gift-giving. And those new outfits we wear each year? This tradition dates from a time when a new suit of clothes once each year was about as much as the average person could afford. This new outfit became your Sunday best, reserved for church and other solemn occasions, while last year's suit became your everyday clothes (or maybe someone else's Sunday best, in larger, poorer families).

The spirit behind all of these traditions is Jesus'. We wear our best to church because we give our best to God. We give gifts to others because we recognize that others often have needs they cannot meet and are too ashamed to express. We decorate our homes to remind ourselves of all the season's joy—the bounty of nature, the beauty in simple things. When we pursue these things with our focus on Jesus, we will find them peaceful, life-giving, and manageable. Give gifts that acknowledge the uniqueness of each person and help them become even more themselves—pastels for the artist, sheet music for the musician, tools for the craftsperson. Remember that home decorating is not an Olympic event or a competition with the neighbors. Choose decorations that bring joy to you and your family and make decking the halls a group effort. And don't worry about the outfit. Children look as adorable in play clothes as they do in little suits and lacy dresses and your friends and family want to see *you*, not what you're wearing.

This Christmas, make sure that Jesus is the reason for your season so that when he's in his crib on Christmas morning, he'll look right at home.

CHAPTER TWO

Mary

The angel said to her, "Do not be afraid, Mary, for you have found favor with God. And now, you will conceive in your womb and bear a son, and you will name him Jesus. He will be great, and will be called the Son of the Most High, and the Lord God will give to him the throne of his ancestor David. He will reign over the house of Jacob forever, and of his kingdom there will be no end."... Then Mary said, "Here am I, the servant of the Lord; let it be with me according to your word."

—Luke 1:30–34, 38

*M*y mother, mother of seven, had inherited from her own mother (of ten) a beautiful statue of Mary. It was one of the few objects in our home that was kept out of the reach of us youngsters. When I was very young, I asked my mother why the statue was so special and she responded simply that Mary was the perfect role model for every mother. When I was a bit older and she in a darker mood, the response to the same question was, "Because if I wanted to imitate Jesus in dealing with the Animals (her pet name for my five brothers) I'd need to be able to perform an exorcism. Some days it's all I can do to ponder these things quietly in my heart."

Now, with four children of my own, I understand both her sentiments perfectly. I can relate to the image of Mary bent over her infant son in the Christmas crèche, marveling at this new life. But unlike that most perfect of mothers, I can well imagine what would fill my thoughts if I knew that my first moments with my eldest would be forever memorialized in the same way. *Unmarried and pregnant? What will people think? You put your newborn child in what? With all of those smelly animals around? What kind of mother are you?* As it happens, I can relate more than I usually care to remember. I was unmarried and pregnant with my first child at far too young an age—nineteen—although under admittedly far less holy circumstances. And my son's first years were spent in circumstances that might miss the label of "ghetto" only because we received no government subsidy. Poverty was our constant companion. What I remember most is the phrase "not good enough." Wherever we lived, I knew it was not good enough for my baby boy. Ditto for whatever he wore, whatever I could keep in the fridge, whatever toys I could manage to provide. And I knew, and often confessed to his tiny bald head, that I was not good enough to be his mother. But there we were, stuck with each other, and we would have to make the best of it.

This would be one of the many places where the Blessed Mother and I part company. Surely, if any mother was "good enough" she must have known herself worthy of that label. But to be the mother of such a Son? And what was good enough for that child? To be born without an earthly father? To spend his first night on a bed of straw? The miracle of birth is too much for any of us to pretend to understand, but the miracle of this birth was on a different scale altogether Mary did well to ponder these things in her heart.

Francis was full of praise for the Blessed Mother. His preoccupation with the Incarnation meant that the means of the Incarnation—Mary herself—was never far from his mind. As Bonaventure says:

> He embraced the Mother of our Lord Jesus with indescribable love because, as he said, it was she who made the Lord of majesty our brother, and through her we found mercy. After Christ, he put all his trust in her and took her as his patroness for himself and his friars.[1]

Because Francis took the Gospels so seriously, he did not have an idealized vision of what life might have been like for the Holy Family. His own fascination with poverty was a result of that gospel poverty he witnessed in the lives of Jesus and Mary.

> The memory of the poverty felt by Christ and his Mother often reduced him to tears and he called poverty the Queen of the Virtues because it was so evident in the life of the King of Kings and of the Queen, his Mother.[2]

Yet, when we think of the perfect family or of the perfect mother, how often is this the image that springs to mind? We live in a society that promises equal opportunity for all, but despises any evidence that that promise is not always kept. Mothers of large families are not the selfless heroines of a few generations past, but irresponsible women who refuse to control either their urges or their biology. The message our society offers is that, if you can't afford children (and this means the best schools, the finest health care, yearly vacations, a lovely home, at least four years of college, and a storybook wedding), don't have them.

Even at a time when such materialism was beyond everyone's reach, Jesus could not have arrived in our world had his mother listened to such a message. She could not provide for him the most essential security of childhood—a father. What right had she to say yes in such a situation?

Fortunately for us, Mary was not in the habit of conformity. Her focus was on God. She was so single-minded in this that she could hear that angel's voice asking the impossible of her. She was so committed that she said yes, knowing full well that she was endangering her own life. And she was so faithful that she brought this infant into the world, raised him to adulthood, and stood by his side while he was tortured and executed. Though Mary's role in the life of Jesus is often described as the faithful yes of an inspired moment, it was, like all motherhood, the work of a lifetime. As Alfred McBride explains:

Mary passed on to Jesus his physical features.... Her motherhood went beyond that as she formed his human character. Mary trained and educated him as any mother brings up a child. Her virtues would have an impact on him. All of us realized that our mother's influence is recognizable in us and we can reasonably conclude that Mary's influence was evident in Jesus.

Mary was more than merely the biological mother of the Lord Jesus. Mary's task in the Incarnation was not over after the event in the stable at Bethlehem. Birth was followed by education. Mary exercised a continuous formation of the young Jesus as he grew from infancy to childhood to the teen years to young manhood.

The New Testament does not tell us how this happened. There is only one brief glimpse...in the narrative of the losing and finding of the boy Jesus in the temple. Mary acts like a typical mother, with the emotions of loss and anxiety and with the maternal demand to know why her son would go off without telling her and Joseph.

It is interesting that Luke cites her words and not Joseph's. "Son, why have you done this to us? Your father and I have been looking for you with great anxiety" (2:48).

These are words we expect a mother to say. Mary is not shy about asserting her maternal authority. It flows from her love of course....

Aside from this brief anecdote, we know nothing else about what happened between mother and son all those years. Her maternal training style, her motherly witness of virtues, her approach to parenting is not recorded for us. Nonetheless, we should not forget that it happened. Mary was indeed mother of God. But she was also a human mother of a son who had a human upbringing.[3]

A good part of a mother's identity comes into play at Christmastime. How the house is decorated, whether we make our own cookies, buy them at the bakery, or skip them altogether, whether the children have to wear ties and "hard shoes" for the day—each is a litmus test of a mother's worth. We'll remember always the presence (or absence) of our own mothers at this time and we'll imagine that says something about our worth as well.

The falsehood in all of this is that so much of it depends upon money. Francis learned from Mary's example that money should never be an end in itself and, even when it is a means to an end, it is often a bad end. Francis emphasized instead a truer generosity that ignored self-serving gestures and focused instead on the real needs of others. One time, when some new friars wanted to keep some of their private property upon joining the order, he made this point clear:

> My dear brother, God forbid that we should sin against
> the rule for anyone. I should prefer to see you strip our
> Lady's altar bare rather than have you commit the slight-
> est sin against our vow of poverty or the observance of
> the Gospel. The Blessed Virgin will be better pleased to
> see her altar laid bare and the Gospel counsel observed
> perfectly, rather than to have the altar properly decorated
> and her Son's counsel violated....[4]

Francis believed that a life of poverty helps us to realize what is always true—we do not depend on our wealth or our own power to survive; we are all utterly dependent on God. That should be as true for our self-understanding as it is for our day-to-day lives. What we learn from Mary is that who we are depends on God's opinion—not anyone else's. We cannot choose how society defines us, but we can choose which voice to listen to. Is a new life worth postponing or forgoing our personal goals? Do the children in our lives know that their worth is unrelated to what is under the tree on Christmas morning? Do we ourselves know the same thing?

This Christmas, let's remember that who we are matters far more than what we do. In the crèche, Mary is not braiding the straw into garland, she is simply present and prayerful.

CHAPTER THREE

Joseph

Now the birth of Jesus the Messiah took place in this way. When his mother Mary had been engaged to Joseph, but before they lived together, she was found to be with child from the Holy Spirit. Her husband Joseph, being a righteous man and unwilling to expose her to public disgrace, planned to dismiss her quietly. But just when he had resolved to do this, an angel of the Lord appeared to him in a dream and said, "Joseph, son of David, do not be afraid to take Mary as your wife, for the child conceived in her is from the Holy Spirit...."

When Joseph awoke from sleep, he did as the angel of the Lord commanded him.
—Matthew 1:18–20, 24

With the exception of their universally bad fashion sense, every father is unique. What sort of man discovers that his fiancée is pregnant, knows it's not his child, and marries her anyway? A very unusual one.

If Mary had to contend with society's negative impression, Joseph may have had an even rougher road. The stories about his life before Mary are wildly different. There is an apocryphal tale that he was an elderly widower, with grown children, who was magically chosen to be the husband of Mary. There is more than one Hollywood version painting him as a handsome young man utterly devastated by the seeming betrayal of his betrothed. The Gospel writers, knowing that people will have questions about this very matter, take the time to explain Joseph's decision to marry: God made him.

Under the law of the time, Joseph had a couple of honorable ways to deal with the discovery of Mary's pregnancy. He could publicly denounce her and have her stoned (which might seem extreme until you think of any jilted lover you have ever known), or he could quietly dissolve their betrothal and leave her to whatever consequences might befall her. Marrying her anyway was not one of these honorable options.

Since the Gospels describe Joseph as a "just" man, we know that doing the right thing was important to him. Since he favored the latter of the two honorable options, we might infer that he was also a kind man, or a man very much in love who wanted no harm to come to Mary, no matter what she had done.

Much like his namesake in the Old Testament, though, Joseph was given to dreams. After his decision to "put Mary away" quietly, an angel explains the situation to him. I can't imagine what it is like to be a man in such a situation, but I don't think I would be appreciably more comforted by knowing that my intended was carrying the Messiah and that I would be responsible for caring for both of them. Like his bride-to-be, though, Joseph was focused on God. He did not follow what his tradition (and probably his friends and family) told him, nor did he follow his own heart. He listened for God's guidance and, having received it, acted accordingly.

The Gospels record a few instances of Joseph in Jesus' life—at the Nativity, the flight into Egypt (the result of another dream), the finding in the Temple—but not enough to give us a sense of who the man was. We know that he was a carpenter and that he must have provided for his family's material needs. Despite their intimate acquaintance with poverty, we don't see Jesus or Mary wandering homeless for long stretches, or lacking food or clothing. Like many providers, Joseph's work is invisible. Did he take the young Jesus with him to the marketplace to trade? Did he pass on his carpentry skills? How did he cope with raising this special child he knew was not his son?

Francis' own father might be a bit more familiar to us. His understanding of justice was a bit more practical—he once brought Francis before the bishop of Assisi (an action which would be similar to filing suit against him today) when the young man sold some of his father's valuable cloth. Pietro Bernadone was the very picture of the rising bourgeoisie—a cloth merchant who traveled far to supply his shop, employed many in his dye room, and insisted that his son make something of himself.

Francis' first professional aspiration—to the knighthood—seemed to please his father. Knights needed a lot of financial backing; horses and armor were expensive. But despite his father's support, Francis had little aptitude for this line of work. In one of the many battles between Assisi and the nearby town of Perugia, Francis was taken prisoner and held for a year, until a peace was negotiated.

Despite this setback in his first experience with war, Francis fantasized during his recovery about how he might best achieve the glory he sought. He was already a popular young man, wealthy, generous, splendidly dressed. He had only to accomplish something to secure his place in the world. He still wanted to become a knight. His father still wanted him to achieve that goal or stay home and take over the family business. But like Joseph, Francis was given to dreams. The *Legend of the Three Companions* describes how a dream changed everything for Francis:

> A few years later an Assisian nobleman was planning to start for Apulia on a military expedition which he hoped would bring him money and honors. Hearing of this, Francis was fired with the wish to accompany him and to get knighted by a certain count…. He prepared magnificent equipment; and, though his fellow citizen was a nobleman, Francis was by far the more extravagant of the two. He was absorbed in this plan and keen to set out, when one night he was visited by the Lord, who, seeing him so bent on honor and glory, drew him to himself by means of a vision. While Francis was asleep, a man appeared who called him by name and led him into a

vast and pleasant palace in which the walls were hung with glittering coats of mail, shining bucklers, and all the weapons and armor of warriors. Francis was delighted, and reflecting on what could be the meaning of all this, he asked for whom the splendid arms and beautiful palace were intended; and he received the answer that they were for him and his knights.

On awaking, Francis rose gleefully, thinking, after the manner of worldlings (for he had not yet tasted the spirit of God) that he was destined to become a magnificent prince and that the vision was prophetic of great prosperity. What he had seen spurred him on to start for Apulia and get himself knighted.... His glee was such that people, in surprise, asked the reason of his delight and received the answer: "I know that I shall become a great prince."...

Now it happened that, after the start for Apulia, Francis felt unwell on arriving at Spoleto; and thinking with apprehension about the journey, he went to bed; but, half asleep, he heard a voice calling and asking him whither he was bound. He replied, telling of his plan. Then he, who had previously appeared to him in sleep, spoke these words:

"Who do you think can best reward you, the Master or the servant?"

"The Master," answered Francis.

"Then why do you leave the Master for the servant, the rich Lord for the poor man?"

Francis replied: "O Lord, what do you wish me to do?"

"Return to your own place," he was bidden, "and you will be told what to do. You must interpret your vision in a different sense. The arms and palace you saw are intended for other knights than those you had in mind; and your principality too will be of another order."[1]

Most of us start out trying to please our parents or other role models. It's the reason we learn to walk, talk, and feed ourselves. As we mature, though, our parents' visions for our future begin to diverge from our own. Either we want something completely different for our lives or, like many young adults, we're not sure what we want. There are hordes of self-help books, life coaches, psychotherapists, and well-meaning friends and relatives who offer some opinion on who we should be, but we all want that voice from the sky telling us exactly what to do. Somehow it is helpful to know that even those gifted with dreams and visions can misunderstand, misinterpret, and make mistakes.

A lot of our traditions at Christmas center around family, and this can be the source of as much heartache and frustration as joy. Few of us became the doctors and lawyers our mothers wanted, or followed in Dad's career footsteps. We might have neglected the family alma mater in our search for colleges, or joined the "wrong" branch of the service, or embraced religious or political views that make every family gathering a tension fest.

As much as we love our families, we cannot center our lives on them. In taking Mary as his wife, Joseph was rejecting a vital part of his culture: carrying on the bloodline, raising children—as many as possible, especially if they were sons. Even if his family came to terms with Joseph's decision to marry under such difficult circumstances, they can't have been pleased with the actions that necessarily followed: the flight to Egypt, the lack of children biologically related to Joseph. And Francis' father, the practical Pietro? When he brought Francis before the archbishop, his son renounced him:

> In the hearing of the many who had come together, he said: "From now on I can freely say *Our Father who art in heaven*, not *father Peter Bernardone*, to whom, behold, I give up not only the money, but all my clothes, too."[2]

Francis stepped out of the rich clothes his father had given him and, as far as history records, out of his father's life.

The parallels in Francis' and Joseph's lives tell us that it's OK to make different choices than our parents. In fact, if our choices are based on trying to discern God's will in our lives, it's far better than OK—it's what we're called to do as Christians. But there is still room for compassion in dealing with our families. Our parents were once quite probably in the same situation with respect to their own parents. And our children will not be eager to follow the path we lay out for them. Though we often portray these conflicts in terms of who's right and who's wrong, we would be better served to remember that each person is unique and what is right for each person will also be unique.

God will not call another man to play foster father to his son. And if everyone were to don beggars' clothes and follow the example of Francis, there would be no one from whom to beg. We must find a way to be the men and women God created us to be, and to encourage and respect that same struggle in everyone around us.

This Christmas, celebrate the uniqueness of each person in your life and do so in your own unique way.

CHAPTER FOUR

The Shepherds

[T]he shepherds said to one another, "Let us go now to Bethlehem and see this thing that has taken place, which the Lord has made known to us." So they went with haste and found Mary and Joseph, and the child lying in the manger. When they saw this, they made known what had been told them about this child; and all who heard it were amazed at what the shepherds told them.... The shepherds returned, glorifying and praising God for all they had heard and seen, as it had been told them.

—Luke 2:15–18, 20

*T*he people of first-century Palestine lived closer to the earth than most of us do today. They were familiar with the cycles of planting and harvest; they knew how to dig wells and draw water. They had to be more in tune with the natural world, since a change in the weather could be a matter of life and death. Thus, the Gospels are filled with fishermen, vinedressers, and shepherds.

Jesus often made reference to this wealth of knowledge when he crafted his parables. Unfortunately, we sometimes miss the meaning behind the stories because we don't understand how absurd these stories must have sounded to his listeners. Perhaps the most outlandish is the parable of the Good Shepherd.

In this story, Jesus relates how a shepherd left ninety-nine sheep to go in search of one who was lost. Even if you have no experience with sheep, a moment's reflection will remind you that they're not famous for their organizational principles. Shepherds are necessary for a reason—there are predators and thieves, yes, but sheep tend to wander. A shepherd who left ninety-nine in search of one would likely return to the fold only to have to repeat the task ninety-nine times. And a shepherd who would lay down his life for his sheep? Well, that's just ridiculous.

Francis was not so removed from the agrarian lifestyle of Jesus' listeners that the deeper meaning of this parable was lost on him. In fact, as he so often did, Francis took this understanding a step further in telling his brothers how far they'd strayed from their heavenly example.

In his *Admonition Six* [Francis] provides a concrete description of what it means to follow Christ, the Good Shepherd. In his view, those who wish to glorify God must be willing to sacrifice their lives:

Let all of us, brothers, look to the good shepherd who suffered the passion of the cross to save his sheep. The sheep of the Lord followed him in tribulation and persecution, in insult and hunger, in infirmity and temptation, and in everything else, and they have received everlasting life from the Lord because of these things. Therefore, it is a great shame for us, servants of God, that while the saints actually did such things, we wish to receive glory and honor by merely recounting their deeds.[1]

Francis places his brothers in the same position as those first shepherds. They received the good news, announced to them by angels. They went to investigate the matter, and repeated to those present what the angels had said. Then they went back to their flocks and fields, praising God. No doubt those shepherds had much to celebrate—imagine those angel voices, that incomparable sight.

But there is a reason why shepherds are an option in our Nativity scenes. They're not quite central to the story. They are not the Incarnate One, who has humbled himself to save the world. They are not his mother, by whose *fiat* all these things were set in motion. They are not Joseph, whose dreams led him to devote his life to protecting this mother and child.

The shepherds, in many ways, are us. We've heard the joyful news. We've taken the time to learn a little more about our faith, to get closer to these holy mysteries. Perhaps we've shared a bit of what we've heard with those in our circle. Almost certainly we've learned to praise God for this great gift. But how would salvation history read differently if we were not in the picture?

The pragmatist would answer that one run-of-the-mill Christian matters very little in the great scheme of things. But Jesus has a different answer. Remember that one lost little sheep? The Good Shepherd decides that that one is as important as the ninety-nine who did not stray. In fact, the Good Shepherd ultimately decides that even that one lost sheep is worth sacrificing his own life.

In holding to this view, Jesus was endorsing an ancient Jewish maxim, later codified in the Babylonian Talmud: "Whoever destroys a soul, it is as if he destroyed the entire world. And whoever saves a life, it is as if he saved an entire world."

Francis saw at once that we are not the star players in the drama of salvation, but that no one is expendable. We must be humble enough to recognize that we are not the center of the universe, but faithful enough to know that God frequently acts as though we are.

This Christmas, remember those at the margins of your world—a friend or relative with whom you've lost touch, a neighbor with no family to share the holiday with, the sick, the poor, the lonely. Do what you can to help someone remember how special they are.

CHAPTER FIVE

The Magi

In the time of King Herod, after Jesus was born in Bethlehem of Judea, wise men from the East came to Jerusalem, asking, "Where is the child who has been born king of the Jews? For we observed his star at its rising, and have come to pay him homage." When King Herod heard this, he was frightened, and all Jerusalem with him; and calling together all the chief priests and scribes of the people, he inquired of them where the Messiah was to be born. They told him, "In Bethlehem of Judea; for so it has been written by the prophet:

'And you, Bethlehem, in the land of Judah,
are by no means least among the rulers of Judah;
for from you shall come a ruler
who is to shepherd my people Israel.'"
—Matthew 2:1–6

$\mathcal{W}$e live in an age of religious intolerance. This can be hard for Americans to accept, blessed as we are to live in a country founded on freedom of religion. But children in public school can find it difficult to express their religious heritage—prayer is forbidden, religious holidays are stripped of their sacred significance, teachers are chastised (or worse) for sharing any belief remotely tainted with faith. Our workplaces are sanitized, our public celebrations scrubbed, even our Christmas cards are designed to please everyone—even those offended by the idea of Christ. Though it's easy to see this intolerance when we're victimized by it, it can be harder to see where we're guilty ourselves.

Debates are raging across the United States over the building of mosques—in California, Wisconsin, Tennessee, and, of course, at Ground Zero. We are still nursing our wounds from the terrorist attacks of 2001 and all too ready to take any perceived offense offered by Muslims. Meanwhile, we find ourselves incredulous that the followers of Islam can't "get over" the Crusades, or that some

Jews are still a bit wary due to their experience in the Inquisition. Certainly, followers of every religion in every age have fallen well short of the principles they espouse. Catholic writer G.K. Chesterton put it succinctly when he said that Christianity had not been tried and found wanting, but had been wanted and never tried.

But in Francis' day, ecumenism had not yet been invented. There was a Crusade being waged most of his lifetime—the Third Crusade having started when he was just seven and the Fifth ending five years before his death. The infamous Children's Crusade roughly coincided with Francis and Clare founding their religious orders. Surely this man, who once wanted nothing more than to be a knight, would understand and forgive our strong religious opinions?

Certainly Francis found himself formed by the opinions of his time and culture, just as we do. So it was that he conceived of the perfect path to God: martyrdom.

> In the sixth year of his conversion, burning intensely with the desire for holy martyrdom, he wanted to take ship for the regions of Syria to preach the Christian faith and penance to the Saracens and infidels.... [1]

Words like "Saracens" and "infidels" suggest that Francis might very well have fit in with our culture. But God apparently felt that Francis was not quite ready for this journey: Francis made it as far as Spain and had to turn back.

Not one to give up easily, Francis made the effort again, with surprising results:

> [I]n the thirteenth year of his conversion he set out for Syria, at a time when great and severe battles were raging daily between the Christians and the pagans; he took with him a companion, and he did not fear to present himself before the sultan of the Saracens. But who can narrate with what great steadfastness of mind he stood before him, with what strength of spirit he spoke to him, with what eloquence and confidence he replied to those who insulted the Christian law? For before he gained access to the sultan, though he was captured by the sultan's soldiers, was insulted and beaten, still he was not frightened; he did not fear the threats of torture and, when death was threatened, he did not grow pale. But though he was treated shamefully by many who were quite hostile and hateful toward him, he was nevertheless received very honorably

by the sultan. The sultan honored him as much as he was able, and having given him many gifts, he tried to bend Francis' mind toward the riches of the world. But when he saw that Francis most vigorously despised all these things as so much dung, he was filled with the greatest admiration, and he looked upon him as a man different from all others. He was deeply moved by his words and he listened to him very willingly. Still, in all these things the Lord did not fulfill Francis' desire for martyrdom, reserving for him the prerogative of a singular grace.[2]

Somehow, in the midst of the Crusades, this sincere Christian and this devout Muslim—Sultan Malik al-Kamil—found that their religious devotion made them more alike than different, and began a friendship as famous as it was unique in its day.

The Magi memorialized in our Nativity scenes were from the East—quite likely Persia. Their interest in and knowledge of the stars, and the term *magi* itself, makes it likely that they were priests of the cult of Zoroaster. Though Matthew doesn't say how many of these wise men made the famous trek, the number three seems to have derived from the fact that there were three gifts. Some traditions name these men, and Saint Bede formalized the list in the eighth century—Melchior, Balthasar, and Gaspar, or some variant of these. There are legends that suggest each king came from a different Eastern empire—Melchior from Arabia, Balthasar from Persia, and Gaspar from India—and met along the way. Others opine that the men were of three different races, demonstrating that Christ was to be king of all the world. Saint Augustine and Saint John Chrysostom offer the minority report that there must have been twelve wise men to correspond to the twelve apostles and the twelve tribes of Israel.

Of what little we know of them, one thing is certain: They followed their own traditions in watching the stars and were led to Bethlehem, just as Herod's chief priests were able to advise him concerning the birth of the Messiah by consulting Scripture. Though we must know our own faith thoroughly, there is a lot we can learn from others.

To learn more about Judaism is to learn more about Jesus, who grew up in this tradition and who always had the words of its Scriptures on his lips. It is sad that so many Christians fail to learn the stories of the Old Testament. For example, many know the story of Adam and Eve, but few know that the story is told twice in the book of Genesis—with some interesting differences between the two. And many Christians know the Ten Commandments (at least some of them), but few know that these, too, appear twice in Scripture and that Catholics and Protestants can't seem to agree on what they are.

To learn more about Islam is to take lessons in the school of prayer. With the exception of the cloistered, few Christians can match the dedication of praying five times daily or fasting for the month of Ramadan (and you thought fish on Fridays was a sacrifice!). Though carefully noting important distinctions between Christianity and Islam, Pope John Paul II offered this observation:

> Nevertheless, the religiosity of Muslims deserves respect. It is impossible not to admire, for example, their fidelity to prayer. The image of believers in Allah who, without caring about time or place, fall to their knees and immerse themselves in prayer remains a model for all those who invoke the true God, in particular for those Christians who, having deserted their magnificent cathedrals, pray only a little or not at all.[3]

In navigating this sometimes seemingly irreconcilable gulf between faiths—or even among Christian communities—it might be helpful to remember the perspective of Mother Teresa, who said:

> There is only one God and He is God to all; therefore it
> is important that everyone is seen as equal before God
> I've always said we should help a Hindu become a bet-
> ter Hindu, a Muslim become a better Muslim, a Catholic
> become a better Catholic. We believe our work should be
> our example to people.[4]

Just as Francis' simple faith and lifestyle won the heart of the sultan,
we can best relate to people of other faiths by being knowledge-
able, being respectful, and being the best Christians we can be.

This Christmas, make an effort to share your faith without using
words.

CHAPTER SIX

Angels

*In that region there were shepherds living in the fields, keeping
watch over their flock by night. Then an angel of the Lord stood
before them, and the glory of the Lord shone around them, and they
were terrified. But the angel said to them, "Do not be afraid; for
see—I am bringing you good news of great joy for all the people:
to you is born this day in the city of David a Savior, who is the
Messiah, the Lord. This will be a sign for you; you will find a child
wrapped in bands of cloth and lying in a manger." And suddenly
there was with the angel a multitude of the heavenly host, praising
God and saying,*

*"Glory to God in the highest heaven,
And on earth peace among those whom he favors!"*
—Luke 2:18—14

*I*f my own experience is any gauge, most Americans are more familiar with this opening passage from repeated viewings of *A Charlie Brown Christmas*, than from having read it for themselves in Scripture. The same parallel could be drawn with respect to how we understand angels. Television dramas, such as *Highway to Heaven* and *Touched by an Angel*, and films like *Michael* and *Angels in the Outfield* have a way of sticking with us. When you hear the word *angel*, do you think of Michael Landon or Roma Downey? One of Raphael's chubby cherubs? A Los Angeles baseball player?

When they make one of their rare appearances in the Bible, angels don't inspire warm, fuzzy feelings or emit an aroma of cookies; they tend to terrify people. When Adam and Eve are cast out of the Garden of Eden, a cherubim with a flaming sword is posted as guard. In the book of Tobit, an angel accompanies Tobias to a foreign land, advises him in marriage (and surviving it), and returns him safely home. But when the angel reveals his identity? "The two of them were shaken; they fell face down, for they were afraid" (Tobit, 12:16). When Sennacherib rode at the head of the Assyrian army to attack Israel? "The Lord struck down the camp of the Assyrians, / and his angel wiped them out" (Sirach 49:21). When Daniel uncovers the lying elders? "This lie has cost you also your head, for the angel of God is waiting with his sword to split you in two, so as to destroy you..." (Daniel 13:59). With examples like this, we might think twice about putting our children to bed with a prayer to their guardian angel—it's like tucking them in with a nuclear warhead!

Just what are we to think of these fearsome creatures? Author Mike Aquilina offers some reason for courage in his book *Angels of God: The Bible, the Church and the Heavenly Hosts*:

> Angels are everywhere in the New Testament too, just as they are in the Old Testament. But there's a very important difference: In the Old Testament the angels are, in a manner of speaking, superiors; now they are our brothers.
>
> The difference is Christ.[1]

Aquilina finds a great explanation for this assertion in the writings of Pope St. Gregory the Great:

Before the birth of our redeemer, we had lost the friendship of the angels. Original sin and our daily sins had
kept us away from their bright purity.... But ever since
the moment we acknowledged our king, the angels have
recognized us as their fellow citizens.

And seeing that the king of heaven wished to take on
our earthly flesh, the angels no longer shun our misery.
They do not dare consider as inferior to their own this
nature which they adore in the person of the king of
heaven; there it is, raised up above them; they have now
no difficulty in regarding man as companion.[2]

While encouraging, this understanding of angels should be bal-
anced. We can call on their protection, guidance, and support, but
we make a mistake if we think we've domesticated them. Their job
is to get us to heaven, not fetch the dry cleaning.

Francis understood that, like the shepherds, the angels are not
headlining the Christmas pageant. Where we find them, we usually find the message they bring; we need to focus on the message,
not the messengers.

His own famous encounter with an angelic vision caused a permanent change in his life. As Bonaventure relates:

Then one morning about the feast of the Exaltation of the Holy Cross, while he was praying on the mountainside, Francis saw a Seraph with six fiery wings coming down from the highest point in the heavens. The vision descended swiftly and came to rest in the air near him. Then he saw the image of a Man crucified in the midst of the wings, with his hands and feet stretched out and nailed to a cross. Two of the wings were raised above his head and two were stretched out in flight, while the remaining two shielded his body. Francis was dumbfounded at the sight and his heart was flooded with a mixture of joy and sorrow. He was overjoyed at the way Christ regarded him so graciously under the appearance of a Seraph, but the fact that he was nailed to a cross pierced his soul with a sword of compassionate sorrow.

He was lost in wonder at the sight of this mysterious vision; he knew that the agony of Christ's passion was not in keeping with the state of a seraphic spirit which is immortal. Eventually he realized by divine inspiration that God had shown him this vision in his providence, in order to let him see that, as Christ's lover, he would resemble Christ crucified perfectly not by physical martyrdom, but by the fervor of his spirit. As the vision disappeared, it left his heart ablaze with eagerness and impressed upon his body a miraculous likeness. There and then the marks of nails began to appear in his hands and feet, just as he had seen them in his vision of the Man nailed to the Cross. His hands and feet appeared pierced through the center with nails, the heads of which were in the palms of his hands and on the instep of each foot, while the points stuck out on the opposite side. The heads were black and round, but the points were long and bent back, as if they had been struck with a hammer; they rose above the surrounding flesh and stood out from it. His right side seemed as if it had been pierced with a lance and was marked with a livid scar which often bled....[3]

This was the beginning of Francis' stigmata, which stayed with him until his death. Just as we have seen throughout Scripture, an angelic appearance signals some dramatic change. The angel stayed Abraham's hand when he was prepared to sacrifice his son, Isaac, preserving the heritage of the entire Jewish nation. The angel that wrestled with Jacob gave him a new name—Israel— that would live throughout the generations of humankind. And the angels in our Christmas crèche? They announced the biggest change of all—God is in our corner, on our side, one of us.

Francis' desire to be like Jesus in every way extended to his desire to suffer the wounds of the cross. In the same way, our faith should make a permanent mark on who we are and on how we behave. If our Christianity is nothing more than a weekend get-together or a box checked on a survey, it is no faith at all. We must find a way to imitate Jesus in our own time and place, and in our own way. The question we must ask ourselves is not so much "What would Jesus do?", but "What should I, as a follower of Jesus, do?"

This Christmas, let the angels remind you of the great change that Christ makes in your life, and let that change shine through in everything you do.

CHAPTER SEVEN

Villagers

He left that place and came to his home town, and his disciples followed him. On the sabbath he began to teach in the synagogue, and many who heard him were astounded. They said, "Where did this man get all this? What is this wisdom that has been given to him? What deeds of power are being done by his hands! Is not this the carpenter, the son of Mary...?" And they took offense at him. Then Jesus said to them, "Prophets are not without honor, except in their home town, and among their own kin, and in their own house." And he could do no deed of power there....

And he was amazed at their unbelief.

—Mark 6:1–6

*Q*uick! Name one instance of a smart mob!

Stumped? That's no surprise. Villagers are idiots—always have been, always will be. In the movies, we have images of torches and pitchforks or townies offering to prove that a woman is a witch by "building a bridge out of her." In the Bible, we have the story of the wandering Israelites, who got so bored waiting for Moses to finish talking to God that they made a golden calf to kill time—at the foot of Mt. Sinai! Even our vocabulary betrays our opinion—"the great unwashed," "the *hoi polloi*." As we see above, even Jesus, present at the creation of heaven and earth, manages to be amazed at the ignorance of the crowd.

Sadly, once we've finished congratulating ourselves for agreeing wholeheartedly with the Lord on this point, we must take a moment to realize that *we* are the villagers. While we tsk-tsk at the Bethlehem innkeeper who turned Mary and Joseph away, imagine: You're the manager of a fine hotel. It's Christmas Eve, all your rooms are booked and here comes this couple, tumbling out of an old, rusty, let's say, Ford Fiesta. The man looks as though he plans his life according to voices he hears in his dreams and the woman is startlingly pregnant. Are you going to juggle your reservations?

We spend our lives trying to stand out from the crowd—but just a little. All of our efforts seem to betray that we don't really want to *leave* the village, but maybe we'd like to be mayor.

The matter is complicated because, though we claim to live in a pluralistic society, the United States is overwhelmingly Christian. More than three-quarters of the population identify themselves this way. The next largest religious group is the entirely nonreligious, then there are a handful of Jews (just over 1 percent) and miniscule populations of what the writers of *Gilligan's Island* might call "and the rest."

What does it take to stand out as a Christian in such an environment? Well, you might show up for Mass on Sunday—just one-third of all American Catholics do. Or you might read a bit of the Bible once a week—that will put you in the top 40 percent of all Americans. But achieving this sort of minimum requirement isn't likely to impress anyone.

Jesus did not tell his followers to go to church every week—though he himself apparently followed all the traditions of his Jewish faith. Neither did he tell them to read the Scriptures—though he appeared to be able to quote from them quite comfortably. The sort of instructions Jesus left for us will, if followed, drive us right out of the mayor's office and past the outskirts of town. Some examples:

If your foot causes you to stumble, cut it off (Mark 9:42)

Love your enemies and pray for those who persecute you (Matthew 5:43)

Everyone who looks at a woman with lust has already committed adultery... (Matthew 5:28)

[Forgive] not seven times, but...seventy-seven times (Matthew 18:22)

[G]o, sell what you own, and give the money to the poor (Mark 10:21)

And perhaps most challenging:

[D]o not worry about your life, what you will eat, or about your body, what you will wear (Luke 12:22)

As a nation that has participated in twenty wars in its short history, it is clear that we're not very good at praying for our enemies or forgiving those who have hurt us. Far from avoiding lustful glances, we've made adultery something of a national pastime. The economic downturn has caused most of us to believe that we don't have to give to the poor because we *are* the poor. (Note: We are not the poor.) And as to not worrying, ever heard of the insurance industry?

Somehow we villagers have managed to build a huge Christian nation without paying any heed to the opinions of the founder of Christianity—no mean feat! And once we've made this distinction, once we've seen that what passes for Christianity in most of our culture is a pale imitation at best, we have a decision to make. Do we want to be "Christian" in the comfortable, mainstream American way that will ask very little of us and provide the companionship of most of our fellow citizens? Or do we want to be Christian?

Francis was well on his way to becoming the most popular, fashionable Christian of his day when the inconvenient happened: He had an encounter with Christ. Bonaventure tells the story of that fateful day:

> He left the town one day to meditate out of doors and, as he was passing by the church of San Damiano, which was threatening to collapse with age, he was inspired by

82

the Holy Sprit to go in and pray. He knelt there before an image of our Lord on his Cross and he felt great plea sure and consolation in his prayers, so that his eyes were full of tears as he gazed at the Cross. Then with his own ears, he heard a miraculous voice coming to him from the Cross, saying three times, "Francis, go and repair my house. You see, it is falling down." At first, he was terrified at the divine command expressed in these extraordinary words; but then he was filled with joy and wonder, and he stood up immediately, prepared to put his whole heart into obeying the command....[1]

Francis began by repairing the little chapel of San Damiano, begging stones and stacking them. With time he began to understand that his mission was not just to the physical building on the outskirts of Assisi, but to the church throughout the world. The foundation of the Franciscan Order sparked a rebirth in the entire church, the effects of which can still be seen today.

To the eyes of the world, though, this encounter with Christ ruined Francis' career, shattered his relationship with his family, and caused him to live in abject poverty, begging for every meal and dressed in threadbare rags. Though we might imagine a small, medieval Italian town to be an idyllic cradle of morality, a contemporary description shows how familiar it would have seemed to us:

> In the city of Assisi, which lies at the edge of the Spoleto
> valley, there was a man by the name of Francis, who from
> his earliest years was brought up by his parents proud of
> spirit, in accordance with the vanity of the world; and
> imitating their wretched life and habits for a long time,
> he became even more vain and proud. For this very evil
> custom has grown up everywhere among those who are
> considered Christians in name, and this pernicious teach-
> ing has become so established and prescribed, as though
> by public law, that people seek to educate their children
> from the cradle on very negligently and dissolutely....
> Impelled by a fear that is natural to their age, none of
> them dares to conduct himself in an upright manner, for
> if he were to do so he would be subjected to severe pun-
> ishments.... But when they begin to enter the portals of
> adolescence, how do you think they will turn out? Then,
> indeed, tossed about amid every kind of debauchery, they
> give themselves over completely to shameful practices, in

as much as they are permitted to do as they please. For once they have become the slaves of sin by a voluntary servitude, they give over all their members to be instruments of wickedness; and showing forth in themselves nothing of the Christian religion either in their lives or in their conduct, they take refuge under the mere name of Christianity. These miserable people very often pretend that they have done even worse things than they have actually done, lest they seem more despicable the more innocent they are.[2]

Christ makes the same offer to all of us. He doubtless called every one of Francis' contemporaries. Perhaps not in a voice from the cross in a wayside chapel, but somewhere in the midst of their lives. Francis followed Christ. A few followed Francis. The rest found some way to drown out that call on their way to wealth, security, and comfortable lives.

So, what kind of Christian do you want to be? If you think the decision is a challenge, it gets worse. All those idiot villagers that you think you might like to distance yourself from? They're in our Nativity scene because they're important. They're the reason Christ came. Not for the smart, the beautiful, or the saintly, Christ came to save the littlest, the least, the villagers. He'd like your help.

This Christmas, stand out as a Christian by finding some way to help those who don't stand out.

CHAPTER EIGHT

Musicians

Listen! Your sentinels lift up their voices,
together they sing for joy;
for in plain sight they see
the return of the LORD to Zion.
Break forth together into singing,
you ruins of Jerusalem;
for the LORD has comforted his people,
he has redeemed Jerusalem.
—Isaiah 52:8–9

*M*any Nativity scenes feature musicians. There might be horns or harps in the angels' hands, recalling their hymn of praise in Luke's infancy narrative. Some have a troop of earthly musicians, plying their simple, handmade instruments. Occasionally the Little Drummer Boy makes an anachronistic appearance.

Though music—and particularly dancing—are seen as suspect in some religious traditions, Francis was an enthusiastic fan. He built a reputation for exuberant joy that sometimes burst out in songs of praise. Murray Bodo captures Francis' transformation from a vain medieval would-be rock star to beloved troubadour of God:

> Francis loved to sing. It freed his spirit and turned the human voice, so often an organ of selfishness and sin, into an instrument of celebration. How he had thrilled to the songs of the French Troubadours who traveled down into Italy from southern France. Bernard of Ventadour, Pierre Vidal, Peirol of Auvergne. Every time one of these great

singers came through Assisi, Francis would be imitating him for months afterwards, entertaining his friends and delighting in their praise of his beautiful young voice.

Francis so loved this performing that once, before his conversion, he went so far as to have a Troubadour's costume tailored just for him. And he cut a pretty dashing figure, too, for the slight man that he was. He would start walking and acting like a minstrel the minute he put on his parti-colored hose and pointed shoes, the hooded tunic with the lute slung behind. He reflected now how much his dress had always affected his behavior. There was something in the simple tunic he put on that day he left his father that altered his whole bearing, from an important, vain Troubadour of Assisi to a poor little insignificant singer.

But his voice did not deteriorate. In fact, it sounded more beautiful to Francis, because now he was not trying to impress anybody. He was simply giving voice to the joy within him and to the beauty he saw all around him. Whenever he felt his heart constricting again, he would break into a song of joy and praise. Or he would remember a song of the Troubadours whose words he never had to change, so perfectly did they fit his Lady Poverty. There was one by Arnaut Daniel that he especially loved.

Softly sighs the April air
Before the coming of May.
Joy is everywhere
When the first leaf sees the day.
And shall I alone despair
Turning from sweet love away?
Something to my heart replies,
You too were for rapture strung.
Why else the dreams that rise
Round you when the year is young?

Yes, a thousand times, yes! Francis loved that image of himself as a lute strung for rapture. He wanted to stand in the wind of April afternoons and let the Holy Spirit play upon him for all the world to hear the beauty of his music. And in every season he tried to be strung and tuned for the hand of Jesus to play upon His poor little instrument, made perfect and resonant by the skill of Jesus Himself.[1]

Christmas music evokes memories of seasons past with a power that few other genres can match. A mother that once cringed at the thousandth cycle of "Rudolph, the Red-Nosed Reindeer," I found myself disappointed when my adolescents no longer wanted to chime in. A song that my newlywed husband and I altered to "Have Yourself a Married Little Christmas" became bittersweet in seasons of marital discord. And those cursed, multicolored Christmas tree lights that danced in time to the most atrocious midi-synthesizer versions of saccharine carols imaginable—the lights that I finally disposed of with a midnight run to the trash can and a little white lie—were sorely missed when we decorated the tree the following year and my youngest said, "It's nice, but it doesn't *do* anything."

Filled as it is with traditions, it is inevitable that we compare this Christmas with those of years past, or of our childhoods, or that special one at the cabin or on the beach. We become locked into habits that make it impossible for the present moment to break in. When my oldest wanted to have the Teenage-Mutant-Ninja Turtle Christmas special on while we decorated the tree, the answer was simple: "No, *this* (*It's a Wonderful Life*) is the decorating-the-tree movie." My oldest grew up with perhaps too fond an appreciation for Frank Capra as a result and I can't help wondering how my current holidays might be colored had

I allowed the opportunity for memories of amphibious martial-arts experts to insinuate themselves into the season. We have the baking-the-cookies album, the playing-softly-in-the-background-while-the-family-has-Christmas-dinner collection, the (really, quite terrifying) Mormon Tabernacle Choir CD that gets all the air time in the car. We always choose the names for our extended-family gift exchange at Thanksgiving, Christmas Eve dinner is always at Aunt Sue's, and Mass is always at midnight (and no, it doesn't matter that the children are falling asleep and that we've got five hours of "some assembly required" ahead of us). And, just when I think I've got it figured out, something about the life of Saint Francis reminds me that Jesus came on Christmas Day to bring joy to the world, not fascism.

As a young man, Francis, like me, had it all figured out. He had breeding, background, a career path, a future. He was always working a plan, closing in on a goal. But his life really started all coming together when he let it all fall apart. He began to pay more attention to the present moment, to what *is*, than to what might be. And something happened, something that transformed a worldly, wounded prisoner-of-war to the Poverello, the little man of God: joy.

As Bodo describes it:

> When Saint Francis was joyful, he would pick up two
> sticks from the ground and, playing them like a violin, he
> would sing in French his praises of God. This gave him
> so much comfort and spiritual joy that he wanted to share
> his song with everyone. And if there were no humans
> there, he would sing to the animals and nature.[2]

Francis' example teaches us that if we sacrifice the present moment
in favor of building a life, we run the risk of missing out on life altogether. This is especially true at Christmas. We know that this year
will have its deficiencies and that future years are bound to bring
their share of heartache and disappointment. But we also know
that the joy we can find in the little moments of this Christmas
season may be all we have to sustain us in that uncertain future. If
we sacrifice this present Christmas for that future Christmas, we
diminish both.

This Christmas, let your music—and all your holiday traditions
—be flavored by what's truly unique about this year and revel in
the blessed, unrepeatable moment.

CHAPTER NINE

The Star

When they had heard the king, they set out; and there, ahead of them, went the star that they had seen at its rising, until it stopped over the place where the child was. When they saw that the star had stopped, they were overwhelmed with joy. On entering the house, they saw the child with Mary his mother; and they knelt down and paid him homage. Then, opening their treasure-chests, they offered him gifts of gold, frankincense, and myrrh.

—Matthew 2:9–11

*F*or those to whom these things are important, pinpointing the date of Jesus' birth is no easy matter. The local census of governor Quirinius (rather than the emperor Augustus), cited as the reason Mary and Joseph went to Bethlehem in the first place, took place around 6 AD. The reign of Herod ended about ten years earlier. There is no secular record of the Massacre of the Innocents (although, to be fair, innocents have been fairly regularly massacred throughout human history and they don't always make the news).

The simple answer to all these seeming contradictions is that the ancients didn't write history the way we understand it today. They were more concerned with the point of the story—an explanation of a tradition, a moral—than in getting the facts right. This is not to say that there are no facts in these stories (certainly Heinrich Schliemann's nineteenth-century discovery of the once-thought-fabled Troy illustrates the danger of this view), just that they must be read with a discerning eye.

Perhaps the last glittering hope of literalists is the mention of the Star of Bethlehem. If there is one detail the ancients frequently got right, it is often related to astronomical phenomena, though their descriptions would necessarily differ from our own. Joshua's "day the sun stood still" could be a metaphorical expression for what seemed to be a long day or perhaps a record of some atmospheric conditions that served to prolong the daylight. It could be a turn of phrase dropped by an astonishingly prescient ancient because, of course, the sun stands still every day, relative to the Earth. Those who imagine that it records a span of time when the Earth stopped spinning on its axis, only to start up again a short time later, will have a hard time finding evidence for this view in the historical or scientific literature.

The Star of Bethlehem is described as moving. The Magi "follow" it from the East until it stops over the manger. Now camel travel—if indeed the kings had camels, none being mentioned in the Gospel—is quite slow. If the "East" was in fact Persia, the journey to Bethlehem might have taken months. Even this slow pace doesn't quite jibe with the description of following a star, though. And a star that could appear to "stop" over a precise location is probably no star at all.

Roman historians such as Tacitus and Suetonius made note of

a number of comets (our word for *comet* comes from the Greek phrase meaning "long-tailed star") appearing in the first centuries BC and AD, and frequently attributed some significance, whether for good or ill, to their appearance. But comets come into view and then pass out of view. They do move, but they don't stop. There were also a number of planetary conjunctions around the time of Jesus' birth, events that might have appeared to be, or might have been described as, stars. Again, though, skilled astronomers would not mistake an alignment of Mars and Jupiter for a new star, nor would such a conjunction seem likely to direct anyone to a specific place on Earth. The one astronomical event that *could* pinpoint a location would be a meteorite, but I, for one, am not willing to believe that God would be so cruel to Mary and Joseph as to cap off a journey marked by uncertainty, privation, and pain by hurling a flaming celestial rock at a nearby hillside.

So, if the story of the star was not meant to offer us a date for Jesus' birth, might it have another meaning? As usual, Francis has some insight. As Thomas of Celano records of that first Christmas crèche at Greccio:

> But the day of joy drew near, the time of great rejoic-
> ing came. The brothers were called from their various

places. Men and women of that neighborhood prepared with glad hearts, according to their means, candles and torches to light up that night that has lighted up all the days and years with its gleaming star. At length the saint of God came, and finding all things prepared, he saw it and was glad.... The night was lighted up like the day, and it delighted men and beasts. The people came and were filled with new joy over the new mystery.[1]

Our recent history has taken the light of Christmas to a new level. The original candle-bedecked Christmas tree, made popular by Victoria and Albert, has given way to the massive evergreens displayed at the White House, Rockefeller Center, and town centers around the nation. Tree lighting has grown from a small, somewhat hazardous affair, to televised ceremonies featuring the eye-dazzling optics of tens of thousands of lights. Suburban household displays constantly change fashion, from the de rigeur icicle lights of a few years ago, to the goliath snow globes now making a deep impression on passersby, pocketbooks, and lawns. And perhaps the most insistent Christmas lights of all are now those of store marquees, billboards, and sale signs.

Those with a few dozen Christmases behind them have

discovered what Francis knew. The light of Christmas doesn't come from the stars above, the shopping mall, or our own really-quite-a-bit-more-tasteful-than-the-neighbors' decorations. It comes from friends and family gathered, each bringing their own light—a happy memory, a funny story, a bright smile. Whether they're huddled around a small blaze in the fireplace or the broadcast glow of a college bowl game, the people we love are the lights in our lives, especially at Christmas.

We'll still deck the halls, light a few candles, and whisper a few prayers toward the clear night sky, but Christmas reminds us to tend to the fires of friendship, of family, and of community.

This Christmas, let your own light shine by taking a moment to acknowledge some special quality in those you love.

CHAPTER TEN

The Animals

While they were there, the time came for her to deliver her child. And she gave birth to her firstborn son and wrapped him in bands of cloth, and laid him in a manger, because there was no place for them in the inn.

—Luke 2:6–7

*O*ur Nativity scenes always have animals. The menagerie differs with time and culture, but I have seen the obligatory oxen and asses partnered with sheep, horses, camels, cats, dogs, chickens, and rabbits. Once again, artistic license holds sway, because the Gospel writers don't mention any animals—just the manger.

Just as the three wise men are an extrapolation of the three gifts, the animals are an "of course" once the manger is mentioned. In a poor, agrarian society there would be no shelter—whether cave, barn, or lean-to—that wasn't occupied by someone, human or animal. And there would be no straw-filled manger without some nearby herbivore. It says something about our understanding of the character of Joseph (Mary apparently being otherwise occupied), that we never imagine him chasing the animals outside. And it says something about our understanding of animals that they seem to fit right in.

For all we know about Francis, his love of animals seems to be his most famous attribute. We see him accompanied by a few of the small and furry in garden statues, squirrel feeders, and birdbaths, and it's a rare holy card, portrait, or icon that portrays Francis without at least one animal in the frame.

This connection between Francis and the natural world is not one we have to make with a few sparse dots. All of his biographers mention it in some way. One of the most charming vignettes of this type is offered by Thomas of Celano:

> Once, when the man of God was traveling from Siena to the Spoleto valley, he came to a certain field on which a rather large flock of sheep was grazing. When he greeted them kindly, as was his custom, they all ran to him, raising their heads and returning his greeting with loud bleating. Francis' vicar noted with very careful attention of his eyes what the sheep did and said to the other companions who were following along behind more slowly: "Did you see what the sheep did to the holy father? Truly he is a great man whom the brutes venerate as their father and, though they lack reason, recognize as the friend of their Creator."

The larks are birds that love the noonday light and shun the darkness of twilight. But on the night that St. Francis went to Christ, they came to the roof of the

house, though already the twilight of the night to follow had fallen, and they flew about the house for a long
time amid a great clamor, whether to show their joy or
their sadness in their own way by their singing, we do not
know. Tearful rejoicing and joyful sorrow made up their
song, wither to bemoan the fact that they were orphaned
children, or to announce that their father was going to his
eternal glory. The city watchmen who guarded the place
with great care, were filled with astonishment and called
the others to witness the wonder.[1]

Perhaps the most famous of these animal stories about Francis is
the legend of the wolf of Gubbio, taken from *The Little Flowers of
St. Francis*, a collection of stories written about a hundred years
after Francis' death. Terrorized by a man-eating wolf, the town of
Gubbio was besieged by its own fear. Francis was staying in the city
and, taking pity on its residents, decided to intervene. Despite the
strong protests of the people, Francis set out, armed only with his
"very great faith." Encountering the fierce beast, Francis set to work:

Then, calling to it, St. Francis said: "Come to me, Brother
Wolf. In the name of Christ, I order you not to hurt me or
anyone."

It is marvelous to relate that as soon as he had made the Sign of the Cross, the wolf closed its terrible jaws and stopped running, and as soon as he gave it that order, it lowered its head and lay down at the Saint's feet, as though it had become a lamb.[2]

After chastising the wolf for its crimes, Francis offered a truce:

Brother Wolf, I want to make peace between you and them, so that they will not be harmed by you anymore, and after they have forgiven you all your past crimes, neither men nor dogs will pursue you any more."

The wolf showed by moving its body and tail and ears and by nodding its head that it willingly accepted what the Saint had said and would observe it.

So St. Francis spoke again: "Brother Wolf, since you are willing to make and keep this peace pact, I promise you that I will have the people of this town give you food every day as long as you live, so that you will never again suffer from hunger, for I know that whatever evil you have been doing was done because of the urge of hunger. But, my Brother Wolf, since I am obtaining such a favor for you, I want you to promise me that you will never hurt any animal or man. Will you promise me that?"

The wolf gave a clear sign, by nodding its head, that it promised to do what the Saint asked.

And St. Francis said: "Brother Wolf, I want you to give me a pledge so that I can confidently believe what you promise."

And as St. Francis held out his hand to receive the pledge, the wolf also raised its front paw and meekly and gently put it in St. Francis' hand as a sign that it was giving its pledge.[3]

Francis returned to the town with the wolf in tow, padding behind him like a puppy. The amazed townsfolk readily agreed to the pact and, true to their word, continued to feed the wolf (who went begging from door to door) until it died two years later. The tremendous change that Francis had wrought is memorialized in the line, "And the people were sorry, because whenever [the wolf] went through the town, its peaceful kindness and patience reminded them of the virtues and the holiness of St. Francis."

Other snippets of tales tell of Francis freeing doves from the marketplace and building a nest for them, of his preaching to the birds or playing his "violin" for the animals and, of course, of his insistence on their presence at the first Christmas crèche in

Greccio. The hay from the manger was even said to have miraculous properties:

> The hay that had been placed in the manger was kept, so
> that the Lord might save the beasts of burden and other
> animals through it as he multiplied his holy mercy. And
> in truth it so happened that many animals throughout the
> surrounding region that had various illnesses were freed
> from their illnesses after eating of this hay.... Later, the
> place on which the manger had stood was made sacred by
> a temple of the Lord, and an altar was built in honor of the
> most blessed father Francis over the manger and a church
> was built, so that where once the animals had eaten the
> hay, there in the future men would eat unto health of soul
> and body the flesh of the lamb without blemish and with-
> out spot, our Lord Jesus Christ.... [4]

Francis' love of the natural world is easier to appreciate in our age of environmental awareness. Those who once insisted on a "real" tree are now more open to sparing the tree by opting for artificial or replantable options. Gift wrap is more likely to be recycled, and recyclable. And the deep spirituality of our merchandisers inspires them to remind us to remember our pets at Christmas—a stocking of treats for Fido, a bit of catnip for Socks, accessories for the bird, the fish, and pretty much any kind of animal imaginable.

The dark days of winter are a good time to consider our relationship to nature. While children (with visions of snow days dancing in their heads) peer gleefully out their windows when an evening brings its first flakes, adults are more likely to grumble at the plowing, the shoveling, the longer commute, the dangerous driving conditions, and the possibility of missed work. Rather than remembering the sweltering months of summer and embracing the cool weather with relief, we snarl at utility bills and snap when a door is left open a moment too long. Even those with an admirable commitment to physical fitness are more apt to drive to the gym for a workout than venture a walk or run in the slush.

Christmas doesn't have to be a loud, hectic marathon of spending, eating, consuming, and disposing. It could be—it should be—a quiet season of remembering and celebrating what's most important in our lives.

This Christmas, step outside your four walls. Take a walk in the snow, have a romp with a puppy, feed the birds, or marvel at the stars. Remember that the world God created for you is quite a bit nicer than the one you've created for yourself.

Notes

INTRODUCTION

1. *St. Francis of Assisi: Omnibus of Sources* (Cincinnati: St. Anthony Messenger Press, 2008), pp. 710–711.

2. Ilia Delio, *Franciscan Prayer* (Cincinnati: St. Anthony Messenger Press, 2004), p. 6.

CHAPTER ONE

1. Murray Bodo, *The Way of Saint Francis: The Challenge of Franciscan Spirituality for Everyone* (Cincinnati: St. Anthony Messenger Press, 1995), p. 121.

CHAPTER TWO

1. *Omnibus*, p. 699.

2. *Omnibus*, p. 680.

3. Alfred McBride, *Images of Mary* (Cincinnati: St. Anthony Messenger Press, 1999), pp. 77–78.

4. *Omnibus*, p. 682.

CHAPTER THREE

1. *Omnibus*, pp. 893–895.

2. *Omnibus*, p. 372.

CHAPTER FOUR

1. Delio, *Franciscan Prayer*, p. 98.

CHAPTER FIVE

1. *Omnibus*, p. 274

2. *Omnibus*, pp. 276–277.

3. John Paul II, *Crossing the Threshold of Hope* (New York: Knopf, 1995), p. 93.

4. Available at www.ewtn.com.

CHAPTER SIX

1. Mike Aquilina, *Angels of God: The Bible, the Church and the Heavenly Hosts* (Cincinnati: Servant, 2009), p. 27.

2. Aquilina, p. 32.

3. *Omnibus*, pp. 730–731.

CHAPTER SEVEN

1. *Omnibus*, pp. 797–798.

2. *Omnibus*, p. 230.

CHAPTER EIGHT

1. Murray Bodo, *Francis: The Journey and the Dream* (Cincinnati: St. Anthony Messenger Press, 1988) pp. 24–25.

2. Murray Bodo, *The Simple Way: Meditations on the Words of Saint Francis* (Cincinnati: St. Anthony Messenger Press, 2009), p. 29.

CHAPTER NINE

   Omnibus, p. 300.

CHAPTER TEN

1. *Omnibus*, pp. 547–548.

2. *Omnibus*, p. 1349.

3. *Omnibus*, pp. 1340–1350.

4. *Omnibus*, pp. 301–302.